MICHELLE OBAMA

By Amanda Hudson

People We Sho

Gareth Stevens
Publishing

Please visit our web site at **www.garethstevens.com.**
For a free color catalog describing our list of high-quality books,
call 1-800-542-2595 (USA) or 1-800-387-3178 (Canada). Our fax: 1-877-542-2596

Library of Congress Cataloging-in-Publication Data
Hudson, Amanda.
    Michelle Obama / by Amanda Hudson.
      p. cm. — (People we should know)
    Includes bibliographical references and index.
    ISBN-10: 1-4339-2187-1   ISBN-13: 978-1-4339-2187-2 (lib. bdg.)
    ISBN-10: 1-4339-2192-8   ISBN-13: 978-1-4339-2192-6 (soft cover)
    1. Obama, Michelle, 1964– —Juvenile literature. 2. Presidents' spouses—
United States—Biography—Juvenile literature. 3. Legislators' spouses—United States—
Biography—Juvenile literature. 4. African American women lawyers—Illinois—Chicago—
Biography—Juvenile literature. 5. Chicago (Ill.)—Biography—Juvenile literature. I. Title.
  E909.O24H847 2010
  973.932092—dc22 [B]   2009011159

This edition first published in 2010 by
Gareth Stevens Publishing
A Weekly Reader® Company
1 Reader's Digest Road
Pleasantville, NY 10570-7000 USA

Copyright © 2010 by Gareth Stevens, Inc.

Executive Managing Editor: Lisa M. Herrington
Senior Editor: Brian Fitzgerald
Senior Designer: Keith Plechaty

Produced by Editorial Directions, Inc.

Art Direction and Page Production: Kathleen Petelinsek, The Design Lab

Picture credits
Cover and title page: Paul J. Richards/AFP/Getty Images; p. 5: Jim Young/Reuters/Corbis; p. 6: AP
Photo/Ron Edmonds; p. 7: Gary Fabiano/Pool/Corbis; p. 8: AP Photo/Marco Garcia; pp. 9, 37: Jay
LaPrete/Reuters/Corbis; p. 11: Courtesy Obama for America; p. 12: Joe Raedle/Getty Images;
p. 14: Rick Friedman/Corbis; p. 16: Yearbook Library; p. 19: Shutterstock/Zina Seletskaya; p. 20: AP
Photo/Pablo Martinez Monsivais; p. 22: Steve Liss//Time Life Pictures/Getty Images; p. 23: AP Photo/
Punahoe Schools, File; p. 25: Shawn Thew/epa/Corbis; p. 27: AP Photo/Greg Wahl-Stephens; p. 29:
Obama For America/Handout/Reuters/Corbis; p. 31: AP Photo/M. Spencer Green; AP Photo/Charlie
Neibergall; p. 32: Rick Wilking/Reuters/Corbis; p. 33: AP Photo/Jerry Lai; p. 34: Gary Hershorn/
Reuters/Corbis; p. 35: AP Photo/Jae C. Hong; p. 38: Mike Segar/Reuters/Corbis; p. 40: Newscom;
p. 42: AP Photo/Jae C. Hong, File; p. 43: AP Photo/The White House, Joyce N. Boghosian, File.

Printed in the United States of America

CPSIA Compliance Information: Batch #CR019270GS: For further information contact Gareth Stevens, New York, New York at 1-800-542-2595

TABLE OF CONTENTS

Words in the glossary appear in **bold** type
the first time they are used in the text.

CHAPTER 1

At Last

On the night of January 20, 2009, Michelle and Barack Obama stepped onto the dance floor. Michelle wore a long white gown, and Barack's tie matched her dress. A crowd surrounded them, cheering. Many cried tears of joy. Millions of people watched from home on TV.

The couple had been together for years, so they had danced together many times before. This time was special. It would be their first dance since Barack had been sworn in as president of the United States. All eyes had been on the Obamas during the presidential **inauguration** earlier that day. Now it was time to celebrate.

Michelle and Barack Obama share a dance at the inaugural ball.

Michelle's Date

For their first dance, Beyoncé Knowles sang the classic song "At Last." The party was the first of 10 that the Obamas attended that night. Many musicians performed throughout the night, including Kanye West, Kid Rock, and Fall Out Boy. At the final party they attended, the new president couldn't resist telling the crowd, "I have the special honor of being the guy who accompanied Michelle Obama to the ball."

Fast Fact

Michelle Obama has Beyoncé and Mariah Carey on her iPod, but Stevie Wonder is her favorite musician of all time.

Michelle holds a Bible as Chief Justice John Roberts swears in Barack Obama as president while daughters, Malia and Sasha, look on.

Historic Day

With Michelle at his side, Barack Hussein Obama became the 44th president of the United States. It was a historic day that many Americans had dreamed about for years. Barack is the first African American to hold the position. Michelle had worked hard to help his **campaign**. Her own career had always been very important to her, but she put it on hold. She believed that the world was ready for change. She knew that her husband could help change it.

Juggling Act

Michelle and Barack are the proud parents of two daughters, Malia and Sasha. All the Obamas worked hard on Barack's campaign. Still, Michelle did her best to keep their daughters' lives stable. She would not travel on days when her daughters had important events scheduled, such as ballet recitals or soccer games. She always tried to be home in time for her daughters' bedtime.

Laura Bush and Michelle Obama talk about life in the White House.

White House Tour

U.S. presidents are chosen every four years in a November election. The winner of the election does not take office until January of the following year. During that time, the new president is called the president-elect. After Barack was elected in November 2008, the Obamas learned about how the job would change their lives. They took a tour of the White House with President George W. Bush and **First Lady** Laura Bush. Michelle Obama and Laura Bush talked about raising children in this unique home.

Meeting the Voters

Barack's presidential campaign was not always easy for Michelle. She was different from many political wives. She liked to make jokes about her husband. Yet, some people thought it was rude to make fun of a man who was a **candidate** for president. Michelle was used to speaking her mind. At first, voters weren't sure what to think of her.

The Obama Girls

Malia and Sasha are the youngest kids to live in the White House since the 1970s. Both girls love the Harry Potter books. Malia has read the Twilight series with her dad. She plays soccer and dances. Sasha does gymnastics.

The White House has a lot of fun things for kids. It even has an indoor bowling alley and a movie theater. The girls still have to do their chores. They make their beds every day and keep their rooms clean.

Michelle speaks at an event on the campaign trail.

True to Her Roots

It did not take long for Michelle to win over voters. As Americans got to know her, they liked what they saw. She drew large crowds at her appearances, even when Barack was not there. Many people liked her honesty and intelligence.

Michelle had not been involved in politics for very long, but she rose to the job of campaigning. No one who knew her was surprised. Michelle Obama has never backed down from a challenge in her life.

CHAPTER 2

Chicago Girl

Michelle's parents, Marian Shields Robinson and Fraser Robinson III, had grown up on the South Side of Chicago, Illinois. They chose to live and raise a family in the same neighborhood.

Fraser spent most of his adult life working for the Chicago water department. It was not a high-paying career, but it was enough to provide a comfortable living. Their first child, Craig, was born in 1962. Their daughter, Michelle LaVaughn, followed on January 17, 1964.

The Robinsons pose for a family photo (left to right): Craig, Fraser, Michelle, and Marian

Sad News

Only a year after Michelle was born, the Robinson family would face a huge challenge. Her father, who had served in the military and been a boxer when he was young, was diagnosed with **multiple sclerosis**. The disease damages the nerve cells of the brain and spinal cord. For most of the time that Michelle knew her father, he walked with a limp. Later in his life, he needed a cane or motorized cart to get around.

Fast Fact

As children, Michelle and Craig looked so much alike that people often thought they were twins.

Role Model

Michelle learned a lot from watching her father handle his disease. Fraser never let his disability prevent him from doing anything. "If he was in pain, he never let on," she would say as an adult. "He never stopped smiling and laughing—even while struggling to button his shirt, even while using two canes to get himself across the room to give my mom a kiss. He just woke up a little earlier and worked a little harder."

Barack Obama shares a laugh with his mother-in-law, Marian Robinson.

Working Mother

Michelle's father was not her only hardworking parent. When Michelle and Craig were young, Marian stayed home to take care of them. She helped with their schoolwork and cooked dinner for the family every night. When it was time for the kids to go to college, Marian wanted to help pay for it. She went to work as a secretary at the Spiegel Catalog company.

Modest Beginnings

The Robinson family lived in a small apartment on Chicago's South Side. In order to give each of the kids their own bedroom, the living room was divided into three sections. Craig and Michelle each had their own small room. The third section was a place for schoolwork to be done.

Marian and Fraser believed that education was very important. Marian taught both kids to read before they started kindergarten. She also wanted her children to learn how to think for themselves. She challenged them to speak their minds. Every night at dinner, the family talked about their days. Friendly **debates** were common.

Fast Fact

As a child, Michelle's favorite toys were her Barbie dolls and Easy-Bake Oven.

❝We told them, 'Make sure you respect your teachers, but don't hesitate to question them.'❞

—Marian Robinson, on advice given to her children

Michelle's brother, Craig, often joined his sister on the campaign trail.

Early Lessons

Michelle was exposed to politics long before she met Barack. Her father had been very involved in politics in Chicago when she was a little girl. In the United States, there are two major political parties: the Democrats and the Republicans. Fraser was a Democrat, just like his future son-in-law, Barack Obama. Fraser worked hard to make sure that people in their neighborhood voted in every election. Some of Michelle's earliest memories are of going door-to-door to get people to register to vote.

Rising Star

From the start of her education, Michelle was a strong student. She liked school and worked hard. Her parents stressed how important school was. They made it clear that she and her brother should apply themselves and take their classes seriously. They both listened to that advice.

In the sixth grade, Michelle was put into a program for advanced students. The program gave her the chance to start taking French and biology classes at the nearby Kennedy-King College. She was second in her class when she graduated from elementary school in 1975.

66My father would make sure that everyone could get to the voting booth on Election Day— because he knew that a single vote could help make their dreams a reality. 99

—Michelle Obama, remembering Fraser Robinson

Magnet Schools

In the 1960s and 1970s, many Americans were unhappy with the public school system, especially in big cities. Schools with mostly African American students did not have the same quality of books, supplies, and teachers that were found in schools with mostly white students. Magnet schools were set up to help.

Magnet schools had high academic standards and better supplies. They were available to students of all races. These schools gave gifted students like Michelle a chance at a better education.

Michelle Robinson poses for her junior class photo.

The Next Step

Soon it was time for Michelle to choose a high school. There were schools close to the Robinson home, but she decided to go to Whitney M. Young, a magnet school. Magnet schools had been set up in response to the issue of **segregation** in many U.S. cities. Michelle would have access to more opportunities than she would at many inner-city Chicago schools. She would also have to ride the bus an hour and a half each way.

Fast Fact

Ninety-nine percent of the graduates from Whitney M. Young go on to college.

Sibling Rivalry

Though Michelle and her brother were close, Michelle was also very competitive with him. Craig was a good student and a great athlete. Michelle made the honor roll all four years at Whitney M. Young, but taking tests came easier to Craig.

When Craig was accepted to Princeton University in New Jersey, she was determined to follow his example. "I *knew* him, and I knew his study habits," she would say later. "I was like, 'I can do that, too.'"

Fast Fact

Craig Robinson attended the same high school as Philadelphia Eagles star quarterback Donovan McNabb.

The Ivy League

The Ivy League is a group of colleges in the northeastern United States. There are eight Ivy League schools. These schools are known for their very high academic standards. Both Michelle and Craig Robinson attended Princeton University, which is part of the Ivy League. The other seven schools in the league are Harvard, Brown, Cornell, Yale, the University of Pennsylvania, Dartmouth, and Columbia.

CHAPTER 3

Heading East

In the fall of 1980, Michelle told her high school guidance counselor that she wanted to apply to Princeton. The counselor said Michelle's test scores weren't high enough.

Michelle remembered what her parents had always told her. Respect authority, but don't be afraid to question it. She knew that colleges looked at a lot of things. Test scores were only one part of the application. She was right. Princeton accepted her.

Michelle attended Princeton University in New Jersey.

Growing Pains

Michelle started at Princeton in September 1981. She was attending the same college as her older brother, who was a star on the basketball team. The adjustment was still hard for her.

New Jersey was far from home. Many of the students were very wealthy. **Minority** students made up only a small part of Princeton's population. Shortly after meeting her, one of Michelle's roommates moved out. The girl's parents did not want their daughter living with a black roommate.

Fast Fact

At Princeton, Michelle was one of only 94 African American students in a freshman class of 1,141 people.

Michelle Obama appreciates the education she received. She takes time to speak with students and encourage them.

Hitting Her Stride

By the end of her four years at Princeton, Michelle had made a lot of friends. She loved to dance and was known for her great clothes. One classmate says that Michelle was "always fashionably dressed, even on a budget. You wouldn't catch her in sweats."

Fast Fact

Michelle liked to play the piano for kids at the Third World Center.

Michelle was also involved with the Third World Center, which had been set up for minority students. At the center, she was the head of an after-school program for the children of Princeton's cafeteria and maintenance staff. Michelle graduated from Princeton with honors in 1985.

Legal Aid

During Michelle's three years at Harvard, she spent a lot of time working in a legal aid office. The office provided legal help to poor people in the community. If someone couldn't afford a lawyer, the students would help. The work was Michelle's favorite part of law school. One of her former classmates says, "I just remember her being very serious about the work she did, and she really cared about the people she worked with."

Boston Bound

Next, Michelle went to one of the best law schools in the country: Harvard Law School in Massachusetts. Princeton had left her with a lot of student loans to pay back. She knew that going to Harvard Law School meant that it would be easy for her to find a high-paying job after she graduated. That way, she could pay back her loans.

Michelle didn't hate law school, but she also didn't love it. After graduating in 1988, she took a job with a law firm back in Chicago. She was ready to go home.

66She always stated her position clearly and decisively.99

—David B. Wilkins, one of Michelle's Harvard professors

Meeting Barack

In her first year out of school, Michelle was already making more money than both of her parents combined. She didn't feel challenged by her work as a lawyer, however. She wanted to make a difference in the world.

That summer, Michelle was asked to be a **mentor** to a first-year Harvard Law student named Barack Obama. He had started Harvard the year after Michelle graduated. Michelle thought they should keep their relationship professional, but Barack liked her from the start.

Barack Obama attended Harvard Law School.

All in the Game

Marian and Fraser Robinson liked Barack right away, but Michelle needed the approval of her older brother. Craig decided to size up Barack on the basketball court. Craig had been drafted by the Philadelphia 76ers, and he played professional basketball in Europe. Barack did not play at that level, but he had played on his high school basketball team. After they played, Craig gave Barack a thumbs-up. "He was confident without being cocky," Craig said.

Young Barack Obama (center) poses with his basketball team.

Tough Cookie

The people closest to Michelle knew that she was tough to please. She was very focused, and she didn't like to be distracted from her goals. She also thought that most men didn't measure up to her father. "You sort of felt sorry for them," her brother said of Michelle's boyfriends. Craig knew it was only a matter of time before she broke up with them.

Eventually, Barack wore down Michelle. She drove him home from a law firm picnic, and the two stopped for ice cream. It turned into a date. More dates followed.

Fast Fact

When basketball star Michael Jordan came out of retirement in 2001, Craig Robinson was chosen to play in practice games with him.

CHAPTER 4

A Change of Plans

Barack and Michelle spent the summer of 1989 getting to know each other. They saw movies, and Barack met Michelle's family.

But some of their dates were unusual. Barack took her to one of the places where he had done **community service** work before law school. It was in a church basement on Chicago's South Side. Most of the people were young African American mothers who needed help. Barack listened to their problems. Michelle was impressed.

Michelle and Barack Obama have always supported each other, in good times and bad.

Saying Good-Bye

In 1991, Michelle's father died. He was only 56 years old. Fraser had been sick for much of his life, but the loss was still a shock. Michelle and Barack were dating long-distance while he was at Harvard. He flew back to Chicago for Fraser's funeral. "Michelle's head was on my shoulder," he would later write. "As the casket was lowered, I promised Fraser Robinson that I would take care of his girl."

Fast Fact

Barack's father was killed in a car crash in 1982.

More Loss

Around the same time, Michelle suffered another loss. Her good friend Suzanne Alele died of cancer at the age of 25. Michelle was with her when she died. Born in Nigeria and raised in Jamaica, Suzanne had been Michelle's classmate at Princeton. She was smart, but she was different from Michelle in many ways. Suzanne was not as serious. She had always said that Michelle needed to relax more.

Now that Michelle had lost both Suzanne and Fraser, she took a look at her goals. She wanted to be sure that she was getting the most out of her life. She didn't want to stay on a career path just because it paid well. It was time for Michelle to consider how she could make a difference.

"If what you're doing doesn't bring you joy every single day, what's the point?"

—Michelle Obama

Coach Craig Robinson talks to his players.

Like Sister, Like Brother

Craig Robinson has always loved basketball. After two years of playing professional basketball in Europe, he entered a successful career in finance. The work made him a millionaire, but like Michelle, he felt something was missing. In 1999, he was offered a job as an assistant basketball coach at Northwestern University. Despite a huge pay cut, Craig jumped at the chance. He has been coaching ever since. Today, he is the head coach at Oregon State University.

Tough Choices

It was not easy for Michelle to walk away from a job with a high salary. She still had a lot of student loans to pay back. Barack helped her decide what to do. He had never cared much about money. He supported her choice to follow her heart. In 1991, she left her job as a lawyer and joined the staff of Chicago mayor Richard Daley.

Fast Fact

Michelle likes to stay in shape. She can jump rope 200 times without missing a beat.

New Direction

Michelle enjoyed her work with the mayor's office. She was able to help solve problems in the Chicago neighborhoods she knew from her childhood. She liked being able to make a difference. Soon, she would have a job opportunity that would give her even more chances to help people.

In the early 1990s, Barack had been involved with a charity called Public Allies. The group helped young people get involved in community service. The staff asked Barack if he would run their Chicago office. He told them he had someone else in mind. He thought Michelle was the person for the job. He was right.

> **"**This was the first time I said, 'This is what I say I care about. Right here. And I will have to run it.'**"**
>
> —Michelle Obama, on being offered the job at Public Allies

Michelle and Barack Obama pose for a photo on their wedding day.

Tying the Knot

Michelle's career was taking off. She was also ready to get married and start a family. Barack wasn't so sure. Michelle told him that she wouldn't wait forever.

In 1991, the couple went out for dinner to celebrate Barack's passing his **bar exam**. The bar exam is the test all law students must pass in order to work as lawyers. Barack told her again that he wasn't sure about marriage. But when the waiter brought out the dessert, there was an engagement ring on the tray. He had tricked her! Of course, Michelle said yes. The couple was married on October 3, 1992.

Fast Fact

Michelle and Barack went to California for their honeymoon.

CHAPTER 5

A New Life

After they were married, Barack and Michelle moved to an apartment in Chicago's Hyde Park. Barack was working at a small law firm. He also taught classes at the University of Chicago Law School. In 1995, he told Michelle that he wanted to run for the Illinois state **senate**.

Michelle was nervous. She knew the job would take a lot of time. Barack would be spending a lot of time in Springfield, the capital of Illinois. It was a three-hour trip from Chicago.

Michelle and Barack share a moment with their daughters, Sasha and Malia.

First Run

In the end, Michelle supported Barack's run for state senate. In 1996, he won the election.

Around this time, the couple decided they were ready to start a family. Michelle began looking for part-time work that would be closer to their home in Hyde Park. She took a job as the associate dean of Student Services at the University of Chicago. In 1998, their first daughter, Malia Ann, was born. Natasha (nicknamed Sasha) followed in 2001.

Fast Fact

Barack has written two books: *Dreams from My Father* in 1995 and *The Audacity of Hope* in 2006.

Working Mother

Just two months after Sasha was born, Michelle was given another job opportunity. The University of Chicago Medical Center was looking for a new vice president.

Michelle brought baby Sasha to the interview. She wanted the hospital to understand that if she took the job, she would have to balance it with being a mom. She could not spend all day in meetings and work late nights. To her surprise, her future employers agreed to all of her demands. Michelle loved her new job.

Rising Star

In November 2004, Barack was elected to the U.S. Senate. He would represent the state of Illinois in Washington, D.C. It was a great step in his career, but it would put a strain on the family. He would now have to fly back and forth between Chicago and Washington. While Barack was gone, Michelle had to take care of the girls by herself.

Keynote Speaker

Barack was given the opportunity of a lifetime in 2004. He was asked to deliver the **keynote speech** at the Democratic **National Convention**. Thousands of people would hear him speak in person. Millions more would watch on TV. It was a speech that could make or break his career.

Michelle knew how nervous he was. In a way that only she could, Michelle made him laugh before he walked onstage. She told him, "Just don't screw it up, buddy!" The speech was a huge success.

The Obamas bought this Chicago home in 2005.

Sudden Fame

As Barack became more famous, things began to change. People wanted to know more about the charming man who had given such a powerful speech at the Democratic National Convention. Barack's first book, *Dreams from My Father*, had been published in 1995. Suddenly, a book that had sold few copies became a best seller. The sales of the book made a big difference in the Obamas' income. In 2005, the couple was able buy a beautiful home on Chicago's South Side.

> 66Daddy, are you going to be president?99
>
> —Malia, age 6, after Barack's U.S. Senate win

Michelle and Barack wave to the crowd at the 2004 Democratic National Convention.

The Next Step

The idea of running for president seemed like a long shot. Barack was young and had been a U.S. senator for a short time. Then there was another issue. An African American had never been president of the United States.

Michelle had many questions: How would they do it? What would happen to her career? Where would Malia and Sasha go to school? Once they worked out the answers, Michelle agreed. She would support her husband.

Fast Fact

Michelle is a Chicago Cubs baseball fan. Barack roots for the Chicago White Sox.

CHAPTER 6

Making History

The Obama presidential campaign kicked into high gear in early 2007. Michelle realized that she would have to cut back on work. Eventually, she left her job at the hospital. It was a hard choice, but she knew it had to be done. "I can't hold down a full-time job," Michelle explained, "and be on the road three or four times a week."

She knew that her whole family would need to sacrifice. "The way I see it," she said, "we're all running for president of the United States. "

The Obamas take a break from the campaign to attend a Fourth of July parade.

"Secret People"

It was very important for Michelle to keep Malia's and Sasha's lives as normal as possible during the campaign. The girls kept their 8:30 bedtime and did chores for an allowance. Michelle was also concerned about their safety. Early in the campaign, the family was given full protection by the **Secret Service**. Twenty-four hours a day, seven days a week, someone was on guard to keep them safe. The girls called them the "secret people."

Fast Fact

In April 2009, Barack and Michelle kept a promise to get a puppy for Malia and Sasha. Bo is a Portuguese water dog.

Hitting the Road

To become his party's choice for president, Barack had to defeat several other Democrats. His biggest rival was Senator Hillary Clinton from New York. The people running Obama's campaign worried that most women would vote for Clinton. They thought Michelle might help win over women voters. This meant that Michelle had to start making more speeches and giving more interviews.

In the Hot Seat

Early in Barack's campaign, Michelle spoke at a **rally** in Wisconsin. She didn't have a script. She said, "For the first time in my adult life, I am proud of my country, because it feels like hope is finally making a comeback."

The first part of the quote was repeated by Barack's rivals. They claimed it showed Michelle's lack of **patriotism**. It was a lesson for Michelle. Now that her husband was running for president, she had to choose her words carefully.

Michelle speaks at the 2008 Democratic National Convention.

One Nation

In 2004, Barack had made a name for himself at the Democratic National Convention. In 2008, it was Michelle's turn. She stood in front of the cheering crowd at the convention and made her own speech. She told the story of her hardworking parents. She talked about why she believed in Barack's campaign. She told the crowd simply, "I come here as a wife who loves my husband and believes he will be an extraordinary president."

Road to Victory

Barack Obama was the first African American ever chosen by a major party to run for president. In the final days of the campaign, it looked like he was going to win.

Both Barack and Michelle drew huge crowds at their speeches. Many college students and other young people attended their rallies. There was excitement at every campaign stop. Celebrities from Oprah Winfrey to Jay-Z came out in support of them.

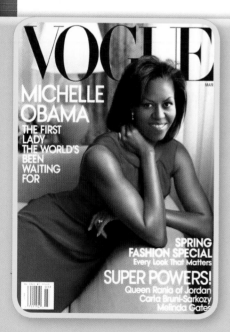

Running For First Lady

As Election Day grew closer, voters wanted to know more about the woman who might soon be their first lady. Everywhere Michelle went, people talked about what she was wearing. They wanted to know about her favorite music and favorite foods. Michelle went on shows like *The View* and *The Daily Show*. She gave interviews to *Vogue*, *Vanity Fair*, *Essence*, and *People* magazines. When she went on television wearing a dress that was still available in stores, it sold out across the country by the next day.

The Obamas celebrate Barack's election at Chicago's Grant Park.

Historic Day

By the end of the day on November 4, 2008, more than 125 million people had cast their votes. Some voters stood in line for hours. In the end, all of Barack and Michelle's hard work paid off. Barack was elected president of the United States by a large margin.

The new first family came onstage in front of a crowd of 200,000 people in Chicago's Grant Park. Many people in the audience cried tears of joy. It was a day that many Americans thought would never come.

Marian Robinson (left) keeps an eye on Malia (center) and Sasha.

Grateful to Grandma

Michelle made it clear that one person made it possible for her to go on the campaign trail. That person is her mother, Marian, who took care of the girls when Michelle couldn't. At many of her campaign appearances, she told the crowd: "Thank God for Grandma!"

When both Michelle and Barack have to be away overnight, Marian stays with the girls. When the Obamas moved into the White House, Marian moved in with them.

First Family

Michelle was thrilled that Barack had been elected. She was ready to take on the job of first lady. As always, her first thought was for her children. "I think the role of first lady is a full-time job," she said. "And my immediate priority will be to make the White House a home for our daughters."

One bonus of Barack's new job is that he works from home. The family has been separated a lot in the past few years. After all the traveling Michelle and Barack have done, they are happy to have the family together in the White House.

Fast Fact

On their first night in the White House, Malia and Sasha were sent on a scavenger hunt. The Jonas Brothers were waiting at the end.

Looking Ahead

Michelle Obama is tackling the role of first lady in the same way she has faced all of the challenges in her life. She has never done anything halfway. She plans to work hard to help working mothers and military families.

She also wants young people to make the most of their lives. She says, "The only limit to the height of your achievements is the reach of your dreams and your willingness to work for them."

First Lady Michelle Obama poses for her official White House photograph.

Time Line

1964 — Michelle LaVaughn Robinson is born on January 17 in Chicago, Illinois.

1977 — Michelle begins attending Whitney M. Young High School.

1985 — Michelle graduates with honors from Princeton University in New Jersey.

1988 — Michelle earns a law degree from Harvard University in Cambridge, Massachusetts.

1991 — Michelle's father, Fraser Robinson, dies.

1992 — Michelle marries Barack Obama.

2001 — Michelle takes a job as a vice president of the University of Chicago Medical Center.

2004 — Barack is elected to the U.S. Senate.

2009 — Michelle becomes first lady when Barack is sworn in as president of the United States.

Glossary

bar exam: a test that would-be lawyers have to pass

campaign: a race between candidates for an office or position

candidate: a person who is running for office

community service: work that is done without pay to help people in a community

debates: discussions or arguments that give reasons for or against something

first lady: the president's wife

inauguration: a ceremony to swear in a public official

keynote speech: a speech that sets the tone for an event

mentor: a trusted adviser or teacher

minority: a group of people of a certain race, religion, or ethnic background who live among a larger group of a different race, religion, or ethnic background

multiple sclerosis: a disease of the nervous system that causes a loss of muscle control

national convention: a large gathering at which a political party officially announces its candidate for president

patriotism: the love that people feel for their country

rally: a large meeting held to arouse enthusiasm

Secret Service: the U.S. agency that protects current and former presidents and vice presidents and their families

segregation: the separation of a race, class, or ethnic group

senate: on the state level, a group of lawmakers from different areas; on the national level, a house of the U.S. Congress, with 100 voting members elected to six-year terms

Find Out More

Books

Bausum, Ann. *Our Country's First Ladies*. Washington, DC: National Geographic, 2007.

Buller, Jon, Susan Schade, Sally Warner, Dana Regan, and Jill Weber. *Smart About the First Ladies* (Smart About History). New York: Grosset & Dunlap, 2005.

Pastan, Amy. *First Ladies* (Dorling Kindersley Eyewitness Books). New York: DK Publishing, 2009.

Web Sites

Ben's Guide to U.S. Government for Kids
http://bensguide.gpo.gov/
Get information about how the government works.

Meet the Obamas
www.barackobama.com/about/michelle_obama
Learn more about Michelle Obama's life.

The White House: First Lady Michelle Obama
www.whitehouse.gov/administration/michelle_obama
Read Michelle Obama's biography on the official White House site.